THE
LITTLE
BEAN
COOKBOOK

THE
LITTLE
BEAN
COOKBOOK

BY PATRICIA STAPLEY

ILLUSTRATIONS BY JENNIE OPPENHEIMER

CROWN PUBLISHERS, INC.
NEW YORK

For Aaron Jupiter Stapley

Published by Crown Publishers, Inc., 201 East 50th Street,
New York, New York 10022

CROWN is a trademark of Crown Publishers, Inc.

Manufactured in Hong Kong

Library of Congress Cataloging-in-Publication Data
Stapley, Patricia.
The little bean cookbook / Patricia Stapley; illustrations by
Jennie Oppenheimer.
p.   cm.
1. Cookery (Beans)   I. Title
TX803.B4S73   1990
641.6′65--dc20   90-33659

ISBN 0-517-57699-6

10   9   8   7   6   5   4   3   2   1

FIRST EDITION

CONTENTS

INTRODUCTION

The Little Bean Cookbook is my gift to all health-conscious, taste-conscious, and inventive cooks — and to their families and friends. It contains twenty unforgettable main-dish recipes that are centered around the dried bean.

Beans are nutritionally near perfect — a superior source of fiber, and the most protein-rich food in the plant kingdom. Dried beans are the least processed packaged food on the supermarket shelf. They contain neither preservatives nor chemicals.

The thirteen varieties I have used in *The Little Bean Cookbook* are readily available at your local grocery store or specialty food store, both in dried and canned form. Canned beans are an excellent substitute for cooked dried beans, so have some on hand for those times when you want to make something wonderful, quickly. Canned tomatoes, too, can be used in place of the fresh tomatoes called for in many of the recipes.

The best way to store beans is in an airtight container in a cool, dry place on your kitchen or pantry shelf. They will keep indefinitely. The longer you store the beans, however, the drier they become and the longer it will take to cook them.

Dried beans, commercially packaged, should be rinsed before cooking to remove any dust or bits of broken beans. If you are buying them loose from bins, carefully pick through them to remove any pebbles or other debris.

Most people have a favorite way of cooking dried beans. This is my tried-and-true method: Place the dried beans in a pot, cover them with fresh, cold water, bring the water to a boil, and continue to boil for one minute. Remove the pot from the heat and let it stand for one hour. Now, drain the beans, discard the bean water, and begin again by covering

7

BLACK   CANNELLINI   CRANBERRY

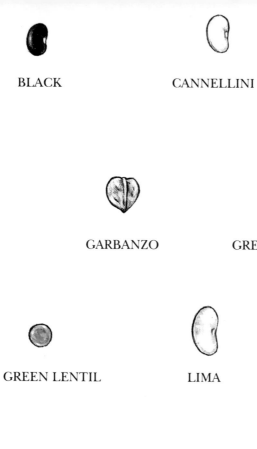

GARBANZO   GREAT NORTHERN

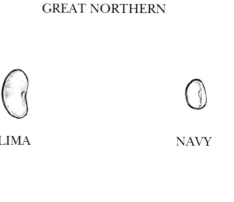

GREEN LENTIL   LIMA   NAVY

PINK   PINTO

RED   YELLOW LENTIL   YELLOW SPLIT PEA

the parboiled beans with fresh water and bringing them back to a boil. Reduce the heat, partially cover the pot, and simmer slowly until the beans are soft and tender.

Keep an eye on the beans as they cook. Add more water if the level gets too low — this means the beans are absorbing the water as they simmer. Do not add salt to the beans until they are tender. When salt is added too soon it will harden the outside of the beans, preventing them from softening naturally during the cooking process.

The size of the bean, rather then the variety, determines the length of cooking time. Garbanzo beans are the largest and will take from two to three hours; cannellini, pinto, red, pink, navy, and great northern need to simmer for one and one-half to two hours; black beans, cranberry beans, and limas take slightly more then an hour; and the smaller split peas and lentils will be cooked tender in forty to fifty minutes.

Nineteen of the twenty recipes in *The Little Bean Cookbook*, begin with precooked and drained beans. When cooking your beans ahead, it is useful to keep in mind that one cup of dry beans equals two to three cups of cooked beans. Leftover cooked beans will keep well for four or five days in the refrigerator, and freeze even better for many months. Plastic sandwich bags are perfect for freezing one to two cups of cooked beans, which you can thaw and use as easily as canned.

At the end of each recipe you will find a chart listing the amounts of fiber, fat, cholesterol, and calories in each serving. Most recipes also have a "Lean Bean Tip," to help tailor the recipe to saturated fat- or cholesterol-restrictive diets along with nutritional information. Whether you're eating for health or for the sheer enjoyment of it, you will discover that the humble but fabulous bean is a joy to prepare and serve.

Black Bean Burgers with the Works

These scrumptious, spicy burgers are sure to enhance any special event, whether it's after the game, after the theater, or as a Fourth of July brunch with family and friends. To keep it light and lively, serve the Black Bean Burgers with oven-baked french fries dashed with salt and red pepper flakes.

Makes Four Burgers

2 cups cooked and drained black beans
1/3 cup finely chopped onion
1/4 cup finely chopped red bell pepper
1 tablespoon diced green chilies
1 teaspoon ground cumin
1 tablespoon toasted sesame seeds
1 tablespoon toasted pumpkin seeds
1 tablespoon toasted sunflower seeds
salt and freshly ground black pepper to taste
2 tablespoons peanut oil
4 slices fontina cheese
4 whole-wheat hamburger buns
lettuce and tomato, for garnish
8 bread and butter pickle slices

11

Place the black beans in a medium-size bowl and mash them with a fork until they are smooth, leaving some of the beans intact. Add the chopped onion and red bell pepper, diced chilies, cumin, sesame seeds, pumpkin seeds, sunflower seeds, and the salt and pepper. Mix well. Divide the mixture into four equal parts, and form by hand into large, flat patties.

Heat the peanut oil in a skillet over medium heat. Fry the burgers on one side until browned. Turn the bean burgers over with a large spatula and place a slice of fontina cheese on top of each patty.

The bean burgers are done when the underside is browned and the cheese is soft. Serve them on open-face whole-wheat buns. Top each empty bun half with a tomato slice, a lettuce leaf, and two pickles.

Lean Bean Tip: Omit the fontina cheese.

Each Lean Bean serving contains:

- FIBER: 2.5 GRAMS • CHOLESTEROL: 0 MILLIGRAMS
- FAT: 12.5 GRAMS • CALORIES: 298

Navy Bean and Leek Regatta in Pastry Boats

Spectacular in both presentation and flavor, these golden puff pastry boats are stuffed with beans and leeks sumptuously sauteed with fresh sorrel and shallots. The nautically correct will want to serve the entire regatta on a large platter, surrounded by a turbulent sea of blanched baby vegetables.

Makes Eight Pastry Boats (Serves Four)

unbleached all-purpose flour
1 pound frozen puff pastry, thawed
1 egg
1 teaspoon water
2 tablespoons unsalted butter
3 shallots, peeled and minced
2 large leeks, trimmed, well washed and sliced 1/4 inch
     thick
1/8 cup chicken stock or water
1 1/2 cups cooked navy beans, drained
1 small bunch fresh sorrel, well washed with large
     stems removed
salt and freshly ground black pepper to taste

Lightly flour a work surface and roll the puff pastry out to a thickness of one-eighth inch. Cut into eight pieces, each approximately three-and-one-half inches square. Place the puff pastry squares on an ungreased baking sheet and prick them all over with a fork.

Whisk the egg and one teaspoon of water together. Brush the top of each square with the egg wash. Cover the pastry squares with plastic wrap and refrigerate for at least thirty minutes.

Preheat oven to 350 degrees. Bake the pastry until puffed and golden, twenty-five to thirty minutes. While the pastry is baking, melt the two tablespoons of butter in a skillet over moderate heat. Add the shallots and sauté for one minute. Add the leeks and sauté until they wilt, about five minutes. Add the chicken stock and simmer until all the liquid has evaporated, about five minutes. Add the beans, sorrel, salt, and pepper and cook just long enough to heat through.

Gently separate and remove the top layer of each pastry shell. Fill the crusty "boat bottoms" with the bean and leek mixture, and replace the top layer at an angle, allowing the filling to show temptingly. Serve immediately.

Lean Bean Tip: Omit two tablespoons of unsalted butter and replace with two tablespoons of extra-virgin olive oil. Omit the yolk from the egg in the egg wash.

Each Lean Bean serving (two pastry boats) contains:
- FIBER: 2.4 GRAMS • CHOLESTEROL: 30 MILLIGRAMS
- FAT: 15.6 GRAMS • CALORIES: 452

Savory Lentil Pâté on Endive

Savory Lentil Pâté will shine on those special occasions when you wish to delight the palates of your favorite guests. It may be prepared in advance and served hot or at room temperature, artistically nestled on a bed of curly Italian endive. For a truly memorable cocktail, serve the pâté with crusty bread, caviar, and champagne.

Makes Nine Single-Slice Servings

2 cups finely chopped onions
2 garlic cloves, crushed
4 tablespoons of butter
4 medium tomatoes, finely chopped
1 cup fresh bread crumbs
1 1/2 cups cooked lentils, drained
1/4 cup chopped fresh parsley
2 teaspoons salt
1/2 tablespoon ground cumin
1/8 teaspoon white pepper
9 to 10 leaves of Italian endive
chopped parsley, for garnish

Preheat the oven to 350 degrees.

In a large skillet over medium heat, sauté the onions and the garlic in butter until tender, about five minutes. Remove from the heat.

In a large mixing bowl, combine the tomatoes, bread crumbs, lentils, parsley, salt, cumin, and pepper. Stir in the onion and the garlic sauté. Place the mixture in a nine-by-five-inch ungreased loaf pan. Bake for thirty to forty minutes, or until the top is golden.

Let the pâté stand for five minutes before removing it from the pan. When the pâté has cooled, place it on a platter arranged with the endive. Cut the loaf into one-inch slices and allow them to lean in a row. Garnish the center of the sliced pâté with a line of chopped parsley.

Lean Bean Tip: Substitute four tablespoons olive oil for the butter.

Each Lean Bean serving (one slice) contains:

- FIBER: 2.8 GRAMS • CHOLESTEROL: 0 MILLIGRAMS
- FAT: 2.7 GRAMS • CALORIES: 165

Venetian
Olive and Bean
Handpies

Create a late-afternoon brunch in rustic Italian style. These flaky, delicate handpies, with their rich, pungent filling, will be the sophisticated and fun-to-eat centerpiece of the event. Round out the relaxed repast with an orange and romaine salad and a light Chianti. Finish with hazelnut gelato and espresso. *Prego!*

Makes Eight Handpies (Serves Four)

2 tablespoons extra-virgin olive oil
1 medium onion, peeled and thinly sliced
4 ounces Italian green olives, pitted and coarsely
     chopped
2 ripe tomatoes, finely chopped
2 cups cooked cranberry beans, drained
20 basil leaves, coarsely chopped
salt and freshly ground black pepper to taste
1 cup grated romano pecorino cheese
basic pastry for a 10-inch double-crust pie
1 large egg yolk mixed with 2 tablespoons water

Heat the oil in a skillet over medium heat. Add the onion and saute for five minutes. Add the olives and mix well. Add the tomatoes and continue to cook over medium heat until the tomatoes lose their liquid and the mixture thickens slightly. Then add the cranberry beans and the chopped basil. Season with the salt and pepper. Cook for a few more minutes. Remove the mixture from the heat, add the cheese, and mix thoroughly. Set aside to cool.

Preheat the oven to 400 degrees.

Using half the pastry at a time, roll out to a thickness of one-eighth inch. Cut the dough into eight circles, using a five-inch round biscuit cutter or bowl edge.

Divide the olive and bean filling into eight equal portions, placing each portion on one side of a pastry round. Pick up the empty side of the pastry and, without stretching it, fold it over to form a half-moon shape. Press the edges lightly with a fork to seal the filling inside each handpie. Gently brush the tops of each pie with the egg-yolk wash.

Place the handpies on an ungreased baking sheet and bake them for twenty to twenty-five minutes, or until they are golden brown.

Serve warm or at room temperature.

Lean Bean Tip: Decrease the cheese to one-half cup. Substitute an egg white for the yolk in the egg wash.

Each Lean Bean serving (two handpies) contains:

- FIBER: 2.6 GRAMS • CHOLESTEROL: 30 MILLIGRAMS
- FAT: 20 GRAMS • CALORIES: 648

Grecian Lemon Bean Soup with Feta Compli

Prepare to enjoy the most delectable of all Mediterranean soups. Its tart lemon flavor is perfect with the delicate pink beans and sharp feta cheese. Serve this exquisite soup with warm rosemary bread, a plate of oil-cured black olives, and freshly steamed artichokes. For the full Mediterranean effect, fill a saucer with olive oil and sprinkle it with black pepper to dip the artichoke leaves as you eat them.

Makes Six to Eight Servings

5 cups chicken broth
1/2 cup raw long-grain rice
2 cups cooked pink beans, bean broth reserved
1 cup finely chopped chard leaves
salt and freshly ground black pepper to taste
2 egg yolks
1/4 cup fresh lemon juice
1 lemon, sliced
4 ounces imported feta cheese, crumbled for garnish

Bring the chicken broth to a boil in a soup pot. Add the rice, reduce the heat to a simmer, and cover the pot. Cook the rice until it is tender, about fifteen minutes.

Add the pink beans and the chopped chard. Cook for an additional ten minutes. Season with the salt and pepper and remove the soup pot from the heat.

Whisk the egg yolks and the lemon juice together in a small bowl. Slowly whisk the egg and lemon mixture into the soup. Reheat the soup slowly, stirring it constantly.

Garnish each serving with a lemon slice and crumbled feta cheese over the top.

Lean Bean Tip: Use an egg substitute for the egg yolks.

Each Lean Bean serving contains:

- FIBER: 2.6 GRAMS • CHOLESTEROL: 12 MILLIGRAMS
- FAT: 3 GRAMS • CALORIES: 168

Oven-Stewed Bourbon Beans

Baked beans are truly an American classic and a staple at many family festivals. Oven-Stewed Bourbon Beans is the one-of-a-kind recipe you might find handwritten in a treasured old cookbook. Ideal for early autumn picnics, this dish would be especially appetizing with a dilled new potato salad, fire roasted corn, and fresh strawberries. Or, you might dress up this dish to serve at an after-the-ball buffet. Simply transfer it to a china tureen and pave the top with a layer of pecan halves.

Makes Eight Servings

2 cups dried great northern beans
1 large onion, peeled
1/4 pound sliced bacon
1 tablespoon dry mustard
5 tablespoons dark brown sugar
4 tablespoons molasses
4 whole cloves
1 teaspoon salt
1/2 teaspoon freshly ground black pepper
1/2 cup bourbon whiskey

Wash and sort the beans.

Preheat the oven to 300 degrees.

Place the onion and half the bacon in the bottom of a bean pot or one-quart casserole. Add the beans.

In a small bowl blend the dry mustard, brown sugar, molasses, cloves, salt, and pepper to form a thick sauce. Pour over the beans.

Place the remaining bacon on top of the beans and add just enough water to cover all the ingredients. Bake, covered, for six hours, adding water as needed.

After about five hours, or when the beans have become tender, remove the casserole from the oven and stir in the bourbon, being careful not to disturb the bacon on top.

Return the casserole to the oven and cook uncovered for the final hour, allowing the bacon to become brown and crisp.

Serve the beans hot from the oven or at room temperature. You may prepare this dish ahead and reheat it, if you wish, by returning the casserole to a 350 degree oven for about thirty minutes.

Lean Bean Tip: Omit the bacon.

Each Lean Bean serving contains:

- FIBER: 1 GRAM • CHOLESTEROL: 0 MILLIGRAMS
- FAT: .4 GRAMS • CALORIES: 274

Bean, Cucumber, and Watercress Tea Sandwiches

Bean, Cucumber, and Watercress Tea Sandwiches add a tempting new twist to a traditional luncheon favorite. Serve these deliciously filled, delicate morsels at a classic Victorian tea party. The ideal bread for finger sandwiches is homemade and one day old, but any favorite bread with a soft, close textured crumb will do well. Bean, Cucumber, and Watercress Tea Sandwiches can also become the canapé delight of any cocktail party. Use your favorite canapé cutters to shape tempting bite-size morsels. The tops can be decorated with sliced stuffed olives, strips of anchovy, golden aïoli rosettes, or pimiento cutouts of hearts, diamonds, or Christmas trees. Let your imagination guide you.

Makes Twenty-Four Tea Sandwiches (Serves Four to Six)

1 12-inch cucumber, peeled
salt to taste
2 cups cooked garbanzo beans, drained
1/4 cup walnuts
1/2 teaspoon grated nutmeg
1 tablespoon brandy
2 tablespoons walnut oil

27

1 tablespoon lemon juice
white pepper to taste
1-pound loaf of thinly sliced bread, crusts removed if
    desired
1 bunch watercress leaves, washed and drained

Slice the cucumber as thin as possible. Very lightly, salt the slices and leave them to drain in a colander for one hour or so, pressing them from time to time to get rid of the excess juices.

Combine the garbanzo beans, walnuts, nutmeg, brandy, and walnut oil in a food processor or blender and process to a spreadable paste.

Sprinkle the lemon juice and white pepper over the sliced and drained cucumbers.

Spread the bean filling on a slice of bread, layer with the cucumber slices and watercress leaves, and top with a second slice of bread. An average loaf of bread yields about six sandwiches, which can be cut into twenty-four squares or triangles.

Lean Bean Tip: Omit the walnuts. Use a bread high in fiber.

Each Lean Bean serving (four tea sandwiches) contains:

- FIBER: 1.8 GRAMS • CHOLESTEROL: 0 MILLIGRAMS
- FAT: 3.2 GRAMS • CALORIES: 398

Garbanzo Fritters with Zesty Pear Salsa

It is the contrast of a browned, crisp surface with a tender layer beneath that makes these fritters so delicious. The nutlike flavor of the garbanzo beans surrounded by a crunchy golden crust is a sensational taste experience. Serve with plenty of Zesty Pear Salsa, a side dish of bright green asparagus, and a full-bodied red wine. These fritters are a snap to make — ideal for a casual meal with good friends.

Makes Twenty-Four Small Fritter Cakes (Serves Four to Six)

1 1/2 cups cooked garbanzo beans, drained
1 teaspoon salt
1 medium Idaho potato
1 small onion, coarsely grated
1 tablespoon all-purpose flour
2 drops hot pepper sauce
2 eggs, lightly beaten
2 tablespoons unsalted butter
2 tablespoons extra-virgin olive oil
Zesty Pear Salsa (recipe follows)

Chop the cooked garbanzo beans coarsely and season them with salt.

Peel the potato, grate it, and squeeze out as much of the liquid as possible. In a medium bowl, combine the potato, onion, flour, and hot pepper sauce. Mix well to blend. Add the garbanzo beans and eggs, and mix.

In a large nonstick skillet, melt the butter in the olive oil over moderate heat. When the oil is hot, drop rounded table-spoons of the batter into the skillet, allowing room for them to spread. Cook over moderately high heat until they are golden brown on the bottom, about four minutes. Turn the fritters over, flatten slightly with a spatula, and cook about two minutes longer.

Serve the fritters on a warmed platter accompanied by the Zesty Pear Salsa.

Lean Bean Tip: Increase eggs to three, but discard the yolks. Omit the butter and increase the olive oil by two tablespoons.

Each Lean Bean serving (five fritters) contains:
- FIBER: 1 GRAM • CHOLESTEROL: 0 MILLIGRAMS
- FAT: 11 GRAMS • CALORIES: 407

Zesty Pear Salsa

If you prefer your salsa very zesty, add extra scallions and jalapeño peppers.

Makes Three Cups

2 Italian plum tomatoes
2 firm pears (preferably Bosc) peeled, cored, and
    diced into 1/4 inch pieces
1 tablespoon fresh lemon juice
6 large scallions, chopped

1 tablespoon jalapeño peppers, seeded and minced
3 tablespoons extra-virgin olive oil
2 tablespoons sherry wine vinegar
1 teaspoon honey

Blanch the tomatoes in a medium saucepan with boiling water for one minute. Rinse them under cold running water to cool, and slip the skins off. Cut the tomatoes in half and scoop out the seeds. Slice them into one-quarter inch julienne strips.

In a medium bowl, toss the diced pears with the lemon juice. Add the tomatoes, scallions, and jalapeños. Mix well.

In another bowl, whisk together the oil, vinegar, and honey. Drizzle over the pear mixture and toss to coat. Serve with a slotted spoon to allow most of the juice to drain off.

Shanghai
Fiery Bean
Lettuce Cups

Fire and ice, this spicy dish is a delight to the senses, and great fun to eat as well. Plan a simple but unique oriental odyssey for your dinner companions. Arrange the Shanghai Fiery Bean Lettuce Cups on a large platter, and accompany with a crusty sourdough bread. Be sure to use red plates, candles, and napkins for that Chinese touch denoting good luck. Select a dry white wine, perhaps a fumé blanc, to soothe the excited palates of your guests, and finish with a cooling ginger-peach sorbet.

Makes Sixteen Lettuce Cups (Serves Four)

2 heads iceberg lettuce
8 dried Chinese black mushrooms
10 fresh (or canned) water chestnuts, diced
1/2 pound raw shrimp
2 teaspoons dry sherry
1 teaspoon soy sauce
1 teaspoon finely minced fresh ginger
1 tablespoon plus 1/2 teaspoon cornstarch
2 tablespoons plus 1/2 teaspoons peanut oil
2 scallions, finely chopped

33

1/2 red bell pepper, stemmed, seeded, and diced
1 1/2 cups cooked black beans, drained
1/2 cup toasted pine nuts

SHANGHAI SAUCE

1 tablespoon oyster sauce
2 tablespoons dry sherry
1 tablespoon soy sauce
1 tablespoon Asian sesame oil
1/2 teaspoon sugar
1 tablespoon hot bean sauce

Separate the lettuce leaves. Select sixteen palm-sized leaves. Some may need to be trimmed so that they are more evenly rounded. Wash, dry, and wrap them in a cloth. Chill for one hour.

Soak the dried mushrooms in hot water until they are soft, about twenty minutes. Drain and squeeze out the excess liquid. Discard the stems and dice the caps. Set aside.

If fresh water chestnuts are being used, peel them before dicing. Canned water chestnuts do not need to be peeled, but be sure to drain them thoroughly. Set aside.

Shell and devein the shrimp, then chop finely. Marinate the shrimp in sherry, soy sauce, ginger, half a teaspoon of cornstarch, and half a teaspoon of peanut oil. Set aside.

In a small bowl combine the ingredients for the Shanghai sauce. Set aside. Combine the remaining tablespoon of cornstarch with an equal amount of water.

Arrange all the ingredients within easy reach of the stove.

Heat a wok or large sauté pan over high heat for about thirty seconds. Add the two tablespoons of peanut oil and quickly swirl to coat the surface of the pan. When the oil just begins to smoke, add the marinated shrimp. Stir-fry until they turn white, about two minutes. Immediately add the black mushrooms, water chestnuts, scallions, red pepper, and black beans. Stir-fry for about one minute. Add the pine nuts and the Shanghai Sauce. When the sauce comes to a boil, stir in the cornstarch and water mixture. Continue to stir-fry until well blended.

Remove the chilled lettuce cups from the refrigerator. Fill each with a tablespoon of the fiery bean mixture. Serve at once.

Each serving contains:

* FIBER. 2.2 GRAMS * CHOLESTEROL: 86 MILLIGRAMS
* FAT: 13.4 GRAMS * CALORIES: 457

Cranberry Bean
and Shrimp
Frittata

This colorful Italian-style omelet can be served hot right from the skillet for carefree dining. If the frittata is left to cool at room temperature, it can be cut into little squares for a tantalizing appetizer, or into larger wedges for a quick and tasty lunch entrée. For the ultimate indulgence serve the Cranberry Bean and Shrimp Frittata in bed with a glass of freshly squeezed orange juice.

Makes Four Servings

1/4 pound medium shrimp, boiled 1 minute, shelled,
    and cut in half lengthwise.
1 cup cooked cranberry beans, drained
4 eggs
1 teaspoon minced fresh thyme, or 1/4 teaspoon dried
2 tablespoons minced fresh parsley
1/4 teaspoon salt
freshly ground black pepper to taste
1/4 teaspoon cayenne pepper
1/2 cup shredded gruyère cheese
1 tablespoon plain bread crumbs
1 tablespoon extra-virgin olive oil

1 tablespoon unsalted butter
1 cup coarsely chopped arugula leaves

Combine the shrimp with the cranberry beans in a bowl.

Beat the eggs, thyme, parsley, salt, pepper, and cayenne pepper together in a medium-size bowl. Add the shrimp and the cranberry beans to the egg batter. Set aside.

Combine the cheese and the bread crumbs in a bowl; toss to combine thoroughly. Set aside.

Preheat the broiler. Melt the oil and butter in a ten-inch broilerproof skillet over a medium heat. When the butter has stopped foaming, add the arugula and sauté until it wilts, about one minute.

Lower the heat to medium-low, and add the egg batter. Cook for three to four minutes, or until the bottom of the frittata is set, but the top is still loose and wet. Remove from the heat and sprinkle the top with the cheese and crumb mixture.

Place the skillet under the broiler and cook until the frittata is golden brown on top, two to three minutes. Transfer to a warm platter or serve right from the skillet.

Lean Bean Tip: Increase eggs to six, but discard the yolks. Omit the butter and increase the olive oil by one tablespoon.

Each Lean Bean serving contains:
- FIBER: 2.1 GRAMS • CHOLESTEROL: 63 GRAMS
- FAT: 18.5 GRAMS • CALORIES: 296

Spice-Fried Bombay Beans with Mango Chutney

Indian food, the most aromatic of all cuisines, is distinguished by its captivating fragrances and intriguing flavors. Spice-Fried Bombay Beans with Mango Chutney is a luxurious one-dish meal that will thrill your guests with a culinary journey to enchanted India. Serve the dish simply with a cucumber and yogurt salad, and a large bowl of fragrant basmati rice.

Makes Six Servings

- 1 pound Brussels sprouts
- 1 large tomato, finely chopped
- 1 teaspoon lemon juice
- 2 tablespoons vegetable oil
- 1 teaspoon black mustard seeds
- 1/4 teaspoon fenugreek seeds
- 2 teaspoons chopped garlic
- 1/4 pound fresh green beans, trimmed and cut into 1-inch pieces
- 2 teaspoons salt
- 1/4 cup water
- 1 cup well-cooked yellow lentils (or yellow split peas), drained

2 tablespoons chopped cilantro leaves (fresh
    coriander)
mango chutney

Trim the hard stems from each of the Brussels sprouts. Cut a deep one-quarter inch cross in the base of each sprout to ensure even cooking.

In a blender or food processor puree the tomato with the lemon juice.

Heat the vegetable oil in a deep pan over a high heat. Add the mustard seeds and when the seeds turn gray, add the fenugreek seeds. Quick-cook for thirty seconds. Add the garlic and cook for one minute longer. Add the Brussels sprouts and green beans and cook, tossing for three minutes.

Lower the heat. Add the tomato puree, salt, and water. Cover and simmer for twenty minutes more.

Add the cooked lentils, mix and cook for ten to fifteen minutes longer. Remove from the heat and stir in the cilantro.

Pour the mixture into a brightly colored serving bowl. Arrange the mango chutney in a smaller bowl to serve as a sweet condiment to the spicy beans.

Each serving contains:
- FIBER: 3.6 GRAMS • CHOLESTEROL: 0 MILLIGRAMS
- FAT: 2.8 GRAMS • CALORIES: 117

Xochitl Mountain Chili with Tomatillos and Nopales

The engagingly piquant flavor of tomatillos give this chili a rich, earthy soul. For a spirited Sunday night supper, set the table colorfully and accompany the chili with a lettuce salad topped with jicama, pomegranate seeds, and fresh mango. Warm a basket of fresh corn tortillas and eat them the traditional way: Roll one up, hold it in your hand, and munch it along with the chili. *Olé!*

Makes Six Servings

1 13-ounce can tomatillos (Mexican green tomatoes), drained
4 whole canned serrano chilies, drained
3 garlic cloves, peeled and roughly chopped
1 bunch cilantro (fresh coriander)
1/4 teaspoon sugar
1/4 teaspoon salt
4 tablespoons vegetable oil
1 medium onion, chopped
4 medium new potatoes, washed and roughly chopped
1 cup raw cauliflower florets
1 cup nopales (canned cactus pieces), drained

2 cups cooked red beans, bean broth reserved
freshly ground black pepper to taste
crème fraîche or sour cream, for garnish

In a blender or food processor combine the tomatillos (include about two tablespoons of liquid from the can), serrano chilies, garlic, six sprigs of cilantro, sugar, and salt. Blend to a smooth puree.

Heat two tablespoons of the vegetable oil in a skillet. Add the puree and cook the sauce for about five minutes, until it has thickened a little and is well seasoned. Set aside.

Heat the remaining two tablespoons of oil in a heavy pan. Add the onion and sauté over medium heat until it begins to soften. Then add the potatoes, cauliflower, nopales, and red beans. Cook another minute. Next add the tomatillo puree, bean broth, and just enough water to cover. Season with black pepper to taste.

Bring to a boil. Lower the heat, cover, and cook slowly until the potatoes and cauliflower are tender, about thirty minutes.

Spoon the chili into individual bowls and top each serving with crème fraîche or sour cream and a sprig of cilantro.

Lean Bean Tip: Omit the crème fraîche or sour cream.

Each Lean Bean serving contains:
- FIBER: 2.1 GRAMS • CHOLESTEROL: 0 MILLIGRAMS
- FAT: 8 GRAMS • CALORIES: 280

Mint-Bathed Limas on Radicchio

Enjoy a light afternoon meal from the deep south — one that is succulent and mouth-watering. Set your table where the sun still shines and serve the Mint-Bathed Limas on Radicchio with melon slices, homemade pickles, brandied peaches, a basket of hot buttermilk biscuits, and spiced ice tea.

Makes Four Servings

1/4 pound small tender green or wax beans
salt
1/4 cup chopped red bell pepper
1 head radicchio
2 cups cooked lima beans, drained
2 tablespoons chopped fresh parsley

MINT JULEP DRESSING

1/4 cup extra-virgin olive oil
1/4 cup fresh lemon juice
1 tablespoon bourbon whiskey
2 tablespoons finely chopped fresh mint leaves
pinch of sugar
salt and freshly ground black pepper to taste

44

With a sharp knife, trim stringy ends off the green beans. Cook in boiling salted water until tender but still somewhat crisp, seven to eight minutes. Drain the beans thoroughly and set aside.

Blanch the red bell pepper in half a cup of boiling water for one to two minutes. Drain and set aside.

In a small bowl, mix all of the ingredients for the Mint Julep dressing, whisking until it has slightly thickened. Set aside.

Separate the radicchio leaves. Rinse, pat dry, and set aside.

In a bowl, combine the cooked lima beans, green beans, red bell pepper, and parsley. Toss gently with the Mint Julep Dressing. Arrange the salad on a bed of radicchio and serve at room temperature.

Each serving contains.

- FIBER: 4.15 GRAMS • CHOLESTEROL: 0 MILLIGRAMS
- FAT: 13.25 GRAMS • CALORIES: 259

Cannellini and Crab Pouches in Roasted Red Pepper Puree

The visual impact of these fabulous little pouches will add that gourmet touch to your next dress-to-kill dinner. All the ingredients — the crêpes, the bean filling, and the garlic and roasted red pepper puree can be made ahead of time, and then assembled effortlessly just before dinner. For the simplest elegance, complete your menu with a spinach, fennel, and pink grapefruit salad, and a spirited California riesling.

Makes Twenty-Four Pouches (Serves Six)

CRÊPES

   1 1/8 cups unbleached all purpose flour
   4 eggs
   1/2 teaspoon salt
   1 1/2 cups 2% low-fat milk
   5 tablespoons unsalted butter, melted

BEAN FILLING

   1 1/2 cups cooked cannellini beans, drained
   6 ounces crab meat, shredded

46

1/3 cup chopped basil leaves; reserve 2 tablespoons for
    garnish
juice of 1 small lemon
zest of 1 small lemon
36 whole chives

GARLIC AND ROASTED RED PEPPER PUREE

3 medium red bell peppers
2 tablespoons unsalted butter
6 garlic cloves
1/4 teaspoon salt
freshly ground black pepper to taste
3 tablespoons water

Combine the flour, eggs, and salt in a mixing bowl. Add the
milk slowly, beating to obtain a smooth, thin, velvetlike batter.
Just before you cook the crêpes, add one tablespoon of the
melted butter and mix well.

Heat a crêpe pan over medium heat. Brush the pan with
melted butter and pour in two tablespoons of the batter. Swirl
the pan to form a thin crêpe about four-and-one-half inches
in diameter. Cook for one minute, then flip and cook the
other side for five seconds. Repeat the process, stacking the
crêpes one on top of the other. Keep them warm and covered
until ready to use.

In a bowl mix all the bean filling ingredients except the
chives. Set aside.

Bring a pan of water to a boil. Blanch the chives for ten
seconds in bunches of twelve. Dry them on paper towels.

Fill each crêpe with a scant tablespoon of bean filling.
Gather the edges of the crêpe to form a pouch and secure the

top by winding it with a chive. Tie the ends together. Arrange the pouches on a plate and cover with a dish towel.

Thoroughly char the skins of the peppers over the open flame of a gas stove or over high burner on an electric stove, until the flesh softens. Place the peppers in a plastic bag to sweat for ten minutes. Remove the peppers from the bag, peel them, cut them in half, and discard the seeds and stems. Dice the peppers.

Melt the butter in a saucepan. Add the peppers and garlic. Gently sauté until the garlic is soft, but not brown. Add the salt and pepper. Add the water, bring to a simmer, and cook, uncovered, for twenty minutes. Pour the mixture into a food processor or blender and puree the red pepper and garlic.

Place four cannellini pouches on each plate and spoon the sauce around them. Garnish with the remaining two tablespoons of chopped basil.

Lean Bean Tip: Omit the four tablespoons of melted butter when cooking the crepes and instead use a nonstick crêpe pan. Use an egg substitute in the crêpe batter as an alternative to the whole eggs. Substitute the two tablespoons of unsalted butter with two tablespoons of extra-virgin olive oil to sauté the red bell peppers.

Each Lean Bean serving (four pouches) contains:
- FIBER: 2.4 GRAMS • CHOLESTEROL: 27 MILLIGRAMS
- FAT: 56 GRAMS • CALORIES: 265

Chilled Red Bean Borscht

Chilled Red Bean Borscht is an unexpecedly rich tapestry of color and flavor. My friend Svetlana provided the inspiration for this vivid ruby-red soup from her homeland, Russia. To create a classic European summer meal, serve this bright soup with smoked salmon, dill biscuits, and a salad of baby lettuces drizzled with lemon juice and olive oil.

Makes Eight Servings

2 tablespoons extra-virgin olive oil
1 medium onion, finely chopped
3 cloves garlic
4 medium red beets, peeled and sliced 1/2 inch thick
1 red bell pepper, seeded and cut into 1-inch pieces
2 medium carrots, peeled and sliced 1/2 inch thick
5 cups water
1 1/2 cups cooked red beans, drained
1 cup fincly shredded green cabbage
2 tablespoons tomato paste
1 cup coarsely chopped Italian plum tomatoes
1/4 cup lemon juice
salt and freshly ground black pepper to taste

sour cream, for garnish

3 tablespoons fresh dill, chopped for garnish

Heat the olive oil in a soup pot. Add the onion and garlic. Cook until golden, then add the beets, bell pepper, carrots, and water. Cover and bring to a boil. Reduce the heat and simmer until tender, about thirty minutes. Add the red beans, cabbage, and tomato paste. Cook for five minutes. Add the tomatoes, lemon juice, salt, and pepper. Simmer for ten minutes.

Transfer the mixture to a food processor or blender, in batches, and puree until smooth.

Refrigerate covered for two to three hours, until chilled. Garnished each serving with a dollop of sour cream and a sprinkle of chopped dill.

Lean Bean Tip: Replace the sour cream garnish with plain low-fat yogurt.

Each Lean Bean serving contains:

- FIBER: 4.3 GRAMS • CHOLESTEROL: 0 MILLIGRAMS
- FAT: 3 GRAMS • CALORIES: 99

Mayan Pumpkin and Pinto Bean Stew

The Mayans were an innovative people and this hearty stew reflects, in a single dish, all the mystery of the Yucatan and its original inhabitants. Rich in a savory blend of uncommon flavors, it is a deeply satisfying stew with a surprising, spicy edge. It makes a beautiful, simple meal served with warm tortillas or jalapeño cornbread, a garden salad, and light sweet flan.

Makes Four to Six Servings

1 teaspoon cumin seeds
1 teaspoon dried oregano
1 teaspoon dried cilantro (coriander leaves)
1 teaspoon grated nutmeg
1/2 teaspoon ground cinnamon
3 whole cloves
4 tablespoons extra-virgin olive oil
1 large onion, diced
3 chipotles chilies (dried or canned), chopped
2 garlic cloves, finely chopped
1 tablespoon paprika
1 teaspoon salt

3 cups cooked pinto beans, bean broth reserved
4 cups pumpkin or winter squash, peeled and cut into
    1-inch cubes
1 pound ripe tomatoes, peeled, seeded, and chopped,
    juice reserved
1 1/2 cups corn kernels (about 3 ears)
cilantro (fresh coriander), chopped for garnish

Measure the cumin seeds, oregano, cilantro, nutmeg, cinnamon, and cloves into a mortar or spice grinder and pulverize thoroughly.

Heat the oil in a wide skillet and sauté the onion over high heat for 1 minute, then lower the heat to medium. Add the chipotles chilies, garlic, pulverized spices, paprika, and salt. Stir well to combine, then add one-half cup of the reserved bean broth and cook until the onion is soft.

Next add the pumpkin or squash and cook until half-done, about twenty minutes.

Add the tomatoes, corn, and beans. Thin the stew with the reserved tomato juice, adding more bean broth if necessary to keep all the ingredients covered. Cook until the pumpkin or squash is tender, about twenty minutes more.

Serve the stew in heavy pottery bowls. Garnish with the chopped cilantro.

Each serving contains:
  • FIBER: 2.6 GRAMS • CHOLESTEROL: 0 MILLIGRAMS
        • FAT: 3.7 GRAMS • CALORIES: 288

Caviar and Bean Salad de Medici

It is rumored that the first beans cultivated in France were given by Pope Clement VII to his niece Catherine de Medici at the time of her marriage to Henri II. This simple but elegantly festive dish says "celebration," and would be sensational at a country wedding buffet or an informal garden party for dear friends.

Makes Four to Six Servings

3 green onions
2 cups cooked navy beans, drained
1 hard-boiled egg, minced
2 tablespoons caviar, black or red (or a combination of
    both)
2 teaspoons extra-virgin olive oil
1 teaspoon lemon juice
1 teaspoon lemon zest
parsley, chopped for garnish

Note: The navy beans should not be overcooked and must be thoroughly drained. This is important, since the caviar will not blend evenly if the beans are mushy or too moist. The beans should be at room temperature before you begin.

Mince the green onions, including some of the tops.

In a medium bowl mix the beans, green onions, and minced egg. Add the caviar, olive oil, lemon juice, and lemon zest. Toss gently to avoid bruising the caviar.

The salad may be served at room temperature or prepared in advance and chilled. For a buffet serving, transfer the mixture to a decorative shallow serving dish and garnish with a small amount of chopped fresh parsley. For an individual serving, arrange a palm-sized, bright-red radicchio leaf on a small plate and spoon the bean salad inside. Sprinkle a line of chopped parsley across the top.

Lean Bean Tip: Omit the yolk of the minced egg.

Each Lean Bean serving contains:

- FIBER: 3.4 GRAMS • CHOLESTEROL: 8.3 MILLIGRAMS
- FAT: 1.7 GRAMS • CALORIES: 128

Spice Island Calico Beans in Tropical Trenchers

Scooped-out papaya halves become colorful trenchers when they are filled with mounds of spicy beans. For the festive calico effect, you'll want to mix your beans for color and texture. Experiment with combinations of kidney, white, pink, navy, black, pinto, garbanzo, yellow or green split peas, limas, or whatever beans you have on hand. Serve the trenchers with cornmeal biscuits and Jamaican rum coolers.

Makes Six Servings

3 green (underripe) papayas, seeded and cut in half
    lengthwise
2 tablespoons extra-virgin olive oil
1 medium onion, finely chopped
2 garlic cloves, finely chopped
1/2 red bell pepper, seeded and finely chopped
4 Italian plum tomatoes, peeled, seeded, and chopped
1 teaspoon finely chopped hot chilies
2 cups cooked beans, drained (use an assortment of 3
    or more of your favorite beans, cooked together)
salt and freshly ground black pepper to taste
4 tablespoons grated parmesan cheese

Preheat the oven to 350 degrees.

Prepare the six trenchers by cutting the papayas in half lengthwise and removing the seeds. Set aside.

In a heavy skillet heat the olive oil over moderate heat. Add the onion and garlic, stirring frequently. Cook for five minutes, until they are soft and transparent but not brown. Add the red bell pepper and cook until it begins to soften. Add the tomatoes and chilies. Cook, stirring occasionally, until most of the liquid in the pan has evaporated. Add the cooked beans and season with salt and pepper to taste.

Spoon the filling into the papaya trenchers. Place them side by side in a shallow roasting pan. Sprinkle the top of each with cheese. Set the pan in the middle of the oven, and pour in enough boiling water to reach about one inch up the sides of the papayas. Bake for one hour or until the papaya shows no resistance when pierced with a knife.

Each serving (one papaya trencher) contains:

• FIBER: 1.4 GRAMS • CHOLESTEROL: 33 MILLIGRAMS
• FAT: 3 GRAMS • CALORIES: 229

Golden Bean and Spinach Dumplings on Wild Mushrooms

The flavor is decidedly Italian but the presentation is haute cuisine. When your favorite mushrooms come into season — especially chanterelles or porcini — assemble a rustic feast around these Golden Bean and Spinach Dumplings. Serve them with an arugula and radicchio salad, very crusty Italian bread, and a deep, rich Italian red wine.

Makes Twenty-Four Dumplings (Serves Four to Six)

1 1/2 cups cooked cannellini beans, drained
1 small onion, finely chopped
3 tablespoons extra-virgin olive oil
1 cup finely chopped spinach
1 tablespoon finely chopped cilantro (fresh coriander)
1/2 cup cornmeal
1 cup grated romano cheese
1/2 teaspoon freshly ground black pepper
1/2 teaspoon grated nutmeg
1 egg white
16 to 24 fresh (or dried) wild mushrooms, such as
       chanterelles, porcini, or morels
4 tablespoons unsalted butter

salt and freshly ground black pepper to taste
2 garlic cloves, finely chopped

Puree the cannellini beans in a food processor or blender.

Sauté the chopped onion in two tablespoons of olive oil over moderate heat until soft, about two minutes. Add the bean puree and cook for one minute. Add the chopped spinach and cilantro. Cook for an additional one to two minutes.

Transfer the dumpling mixture to a bowl. Add the cornmeal and mix well. Then add half the grated cheese, and the pepper, nutmeg, and egg white. Combine thoroughly.

Preheat the oven to 350 degrees.

Bring three quarts of salted water to a boil in a saucepan.

Coat a large baking dish with the remaining one tablespoon of olive oil.

Dip a teaspoon in cool water. Fill the wet spoon with batter and drop the dumpling into the saucepan of boiling water. Continue this process until all of the dumpling batter is used. When the water in the saucepan returns to a boil, cover and simmer the dumplings for two to three minutes. Remove them from the saucepan with a slotted spoon, and transfer them to the oiled baking dish. Sprinkle the tops of the dumplings with the remaining grated cheese and bake for ten minutes.

If you are using fresh wild mushrooms, clean them with a soft mushroom brush or cloth. If the mushrooms are dried reconstitute them by soaking them in tepid water for twenty minutes to one hour. Drain thoroughly, squeezing out any excess liquid. Slice the mushrooms into rather large pieces. If the stems are shriveled or pulpy, discard them.

Cook the mushrooms in two batches; if they are crowded

in the pan, they will steam instead of sauté. To cook the first batch, heat two tablespoons butter in a wide skillet. Add eight to twelve mushrooms and sauté them over high heat for about two minutes. When they begin to lose their juices, season with salt, pepper, and half the garlic. Cook for another few minutes, or until the garlic turns soft. Take the first batch of mushrooms out of the skillet and place on a warm plate. Repeat this procedure for the remaining mushrooms and garlic.

Select a large platter and cover it with a bed of wild mushrooms. Arrange the bean and spinach dumplings on top. Serve immediately.

Lean Bean Tip: Decrease the cheese to one-half cup. Sauté the mushrooms in olive oil, instead of unsalted butter.

Each Lean Bean serving (five dumplings) contains:

- FIBER: 7.5 GRAMS • CHOLESTEROL: 28 MILLIGRAMS
- FAT: 26 GRAMS • CALORIES: 407

Black Bean Soufflé with Orange Liqueur Cream

Add a dash of panache to your party to end all parties. Your very happy guests will not soon forget this sumptuous soufflé, enhanced with a rich, tangy orange liqueur cream. Serve it with a platter of baby vegetables marinated in basalmic vinegar, olive oil, and fresh basil. And, of course, what is a soufflé without champagne?

Makes Four Servings

1 1/2 cups cooked black beans, drained
1 tablespoon minced mint leaves
1 tablespoon grated orange peel
1/4 teaspoon salt
5 egg whites, beaten until stiff
1 cup plain yogurt
2 tablespoons orange liqueur

Preheat the oven to 350 degrees.

Puree the black beans in a food mill or blender with the mint, orange peel, and salt. Transfer to a bowl.

Delicately fold the beaten egg whites into the bean puree, one fourth at a time. Turn the mixture into a buttered five-cup soufflé dish, leaving a space of at least one-and-one-quarter inches between the top of the mixture and the rim of the dish.

Bake for thirty-five to forty-five minutes, until the soufflé rises to the top of the dish and turns a golden brown. Remove from the oven and top with a sauce made by whipping the yogurt with the orange liqueur.

Serve the soufflé immediately.

Lean Bean Tip: Use low-fat yogurt in the cream sauce.

Each Lean Bean serving contains:

- FIBER: 1.4 GRAMS • CHOLESTEROL: 3 MILLIGRAMS
- FAT: 1.2 GRAMS • CALORIES: 148

BEAN INDEX